HOW TO REMEMBER YOUR POWER
THROUGH SELF-LOVE AND FORGIVENESS

SHOW ME

HOW TO
REMEMBER
YOUR POWER

THROUGH SELF-LOVE
AND FORGIVENESS

BY ANGELA BLAHA

© 2015, Angela Blaha
All rights reserved.

Show Me: How to Remember Your Power through Self-Love and Forgiveness

ISBN 978-1-942969-00-6 Print
ISBN 978-1-942969-01-3 E-Book

Published by AuthorSOS
An imprint of Creative Revolutions
Atlanta, GA

This book may not be reproduced in whole or in part, without written permission from the author, except by a reviewer who may quote brief passages. Nor may any part of this book be reproduced, stored in a retrieval system, or transmitted in any form or by any means electronic, mechanical, photocopying, recording, scanning or otherwise.

Library of Congress Control Number: 2015903559

Printed in the United States of America

AUTHOR WEBSITE www.AngelaBlaha.com

Table of Contents

Introduction ix
Why Am I Here? 1
Who Am I? 5
Who Can I Be? 9
A Meditation on Creativity 13
What Is Important for Me to Know Today? 15
What Are Vibrations? 19
Why Does It Matter That I Love Myself? 23
What Is the First Step in Loving Myself? 29
How Can I Remember What Divine Love Is? 33
A Meditation on Divine Love 37
How Can I Learn to Be Enough? 39
How Can I Cultivate Authenticity? 43
What Does It Mean to Be Compassionate? 47
What Does It Mean to Be Vulnerable? 51
How Can I Experience My Power? 55
A Meditation on Personal Power 59
What Else Is There to Know about My Power? 61
Why Is My Energy So Low Today? 67

How Can I Learn to Expect a Miracle? 73
How Can I Find Something in Me to Love? 77
How Is Polarity Present in My Life? 83
How Can I Become Shame-Resilient? 87
How Can I Love Myself When I Don't Know Myself? 91
Why Is My Life So in Flow Right Now? 95
Why Is It We Dislike Talking about Self-Love? 99
What Is the Vibration of a Soul as It Heals? 103
What Is the Root of My Thoughts? 107
How Can I Stop Being So Afraid? 113
What Does Forgiveness Mean? 117
Why Is Forgiveness Important for My Soul? 121
Why Is It Important to Forgive Myself? 127
How Can I Forgive When There's So Much to Forgive? 131
What Else Do I Need to Understand about Forgiveness? 135
How Can I Forgive Myself When I Continue to Mess Up? 139
What If I Know I Have Harmed Someone? 143
What If I Do Not Think I Have Anything to Forgive 147
What Are the Actual Steps of Forgiveness? 151
Next Steps 155
About the Author 157

Introduction

This book includes a series of channeled messages from my higher self, my soul self. I have walked the path of self-love and forgiveness and asked to be shown a new way forward. This is a book for everyone who has embraced a spiritual journey of love and that includes every one of us. It offers support and encouragement as you remember who you are at the core of your being.

I have the privilege of working with clients who are focused on emotional well-being. What I have noticed in my work is how important it is to love yourself unconditionally. Many of my clients believe that forgiveness is for someone else. When we have this belief, we forget to forgive the self and often create conditions for loving the self. When we love ourselves yet create an attachment of such conditions of forgiveness, we hold ourselves back from creating a life of bliss.

I am writing this book to help with this process and to help you understand how important unconditional love and forgiveness is on your human journey. As I continue to use my intuitive abilities, I gain an even more profound understanding of what it means to remember we are from love. With every encounter with Spirit, I am continuously reminded to love who I chose to be in this form. It has become more and more important that I share this information with the world.

The Search for Something Greater

The path to self-love and forgiveness is one I have walked personally. I have very few memories of my childhood. Although I have always felt loved by my family, I knew I was different from them as well. Self-love had been a struggle for me, and I had blamed it on the absence of those early memories.

When I entered college and studied psychology, there were many classes that focused on Nature vs. Nurture which sparked even more wonder about my early memories or the absence of them. To this day, those early memories still elude me; however, I do not focus on them. Rather, I focus on what is now and on knowing who I am and loving who I have become.

I believe we have the ability to choose our lives before we are born into a human body. I know I chose to be born into a dysfunctional family as my family had great lessons to teach me. At an early age I knew the cycle of addiction would be broken with me, and that was the gift this family was to teach me.

Many years later, I see how my early years cultivated compassion and understanding with Spirit. The absence of memory protected me and allowed me to maintain my balance and perspective so that I can now serve in this way.

I grew up in the country. My family were farmers in the rural Dakotas. Back then farming involved intense manual labor, and the idea of feast or famine was quite real. Despite living in a rural environment with little of life's luxuries, family parties were a regular part of life.

Being angry at the world, stubborn, and emotionally weak seemed to be part of the criteria for being a member of my family. I speak of "weakness" though, in my internal wisdom, I am aware it takes a good amount of personal strength to live a life of joy and grace. Living a life

Introduction

according to one's soul path is not something I witnessed my parents doing until they were older, much later in my life.

I always felt like an outsider within the family unit and in society. I used to tell people I was adopted because I felt so different from the main group. My mother told me often that it was okay to be different, all the while not remembering ever saying such words. Again, I witnessed the protection and watch care of Spirit in my life.

During my middle school years, I tried to fit in, but it never really worked. These attempts only brought me more pain and suffering. I have never had close friendships. That was always fine with me as I have never understood relationships in which individuals depend on each other for happiness. Sometimes it was a bit lonely, but I always found things to distract myself with and interests to pursue.

I have spent the majority of my life searching for something greater. For a short time at about age 16, there was contentment and peace along with a strong connection with Spirit and my higher self. During these times, I seemed to have reached some place within me that was so peaceful and full of grace that I really could not wrap my mind around it. I have no words to describe it.

I had no one to talk to about my spiritual journey. In my home nothing personal was talked about. Due to this reality, I quickly dismissed my vast sense of knowing and returned to eating, sleeping, and going through the mundane rituals of daily living. Throughout the remainder of my teens and well into my 20s, this peace would show itself for short durations and then retreat just as quickly as it had come.

Up until this time, I really thought such experiences with Spirit were normal. Finally, the premonitions became so strong I could no longer ignore them. Soon, the fear of the premonitions and the knowing too much became overwhelming, and I asked God to take it all away. Life continued in its mundane chores as a I raised a family. I continued with striving to work myself up the perceived money ladder, only to find myself increasing in pain and suffering.

Short fragments of time were spent in meditation, where I seemed to be able to touch my soul, feeling the vastness of its love. There came a turning point of no return as I watched my parents slowly ascend from their earthly bodies. I began to awaken again, and the feelings of joy and grace returned. It was at this point that I vowed never to return to any other way of being.

You see, I have always known about things that others have not. I knew I would break the cycle of addiction from which the family patterns were created. I viewed these patterns as karmic energies that we bring with us from one life to another. I have always been an intuitive being, knowing that there is more to this life than eating, sleeping, going to work, and returning home again only to repeat the cycle. I have always had a sense that there was something more, and I have searched for this essence my entire life.

I am forever grateful for choosing to come into this life and for choosing this family, for they have taught me much about how to be. I am especially thankful for being a part of the changing of the ages — the Age of Aquarius, as it was known of when I was growing up in the decades of the '60s and '70s. Most of all, I am grateful as I continue on my journey of love, joy, and peace. I am home!

Channeling My Higher Self

For many years I had an interest in learning to channel beings from the light of Source. I would watch or listen to excerpts of Esther Hicks who has always intrigued me. I started to read and read, wondering what it would be like to have such a gift.

Introduction

One day after reading *Opening to Channel* by Sanaya Roman and Duane Packer, I asked God if I could channel a high energy someday. Immediately I heard, "Yes." Much to my amazement, I tried it with a friend, and now I channel nearly everyday. I have channeled loved ones who have transitioned, high guides, and archangels — the list goes on and on.

When I channel energies that make up my higher self, I feel a more expansive presence that is not outside of my energy field; rather, it *is* my energy field. My higher self is me: all parts of me — my physical self, my mental self, my emotional self, and my spiritual self. I can feel a different form of vibration when I move to my higher self versus my logical, everyday self. This vibration of my higher self has a presence that is much calmer, that views everything in a form of natural and logical consequences, and that is very kind, loving, and compassionate.

My higher self is a presence that tries very hard to find the precise words to convey the message it desires to express. As I connect to my higher self, I make an effort to choose words that are common and easy to understand. I try to find words that have the best vibration for expressing a particular message. My higher self finds words that seem to have layers of vibration to them, so that everyone who reads them will expand and grow, no matter what dimension that individual soul has chosen this lifetime.

I see wisdom beyond the human nature when I look at my higher self. I see a never-ending glow of love that leaves me speechless and almost gasping for my breath. I see a brilliant whiteness that desires to spread as far as the oceans and as deep as the galaxies will allow.

Likewise, I hear only words of kindness, words of love, from the higher realms. Often, I channel Archangel Metatron and St. Germaine and these are the primary energies channeled for this book. I often wonder why my physical nature is not more like my higher self. Then I realize that my higher self is I and that we are not separate. Yet, there is a worthiness component of such love, wisdom, and compassion that I do not understand. I do not know where it comes from or where within me it resides.

Somewhere along my life's path I took on the belief that in order to be worthy of such angelic beings, emotions, and feelings, I needed to be angelic myself. Since I am human and was taught that I was born in sin, I never really felt worthy of being among the angelic realms. This of course created self-doubt. I now know that we are God / Spirit / Universe and that to deny such worth is denying we are God / Spirit / Universe. We are not sinners from the beginning; rather, we are what we choose to be and to experience.

My Path of Self-Love

Self-love is a way of being. When I learned about self-love in college, it seemed very foreign to me. It was not a concept that I was familiar with, yet I had a sense of knowing how very important it would be to learn and to become. I believe we come to this life with self-love. Somewhere along the way, it is destroyed or morphed into something different.

Self-love is a natural way of being that can sometimes be perceived as too confident or egotistical. Keep in mind that these examples are simply perceptions, and self-love is intended to be a natural way of being. Once my self-love morphed into doubt, worry, and imbalance, it took some time to regain. I primarily regained my love for myself through meditation, which remains to be a daily practice.

When I love who I am, my life flows effortlessly and my connection with Spirit / God / Universe is easy. In the beginning of my spiritual journey, I would connect with my higher self through meditation and I have included some meditations in this book for you to help you along your journey.

INTRODUCTION

How to Use This Book

You may find value in reading through the channeled messages in the order they are presented. Alternatively, you may wish to choose a new topic each time you pick up the book and read just one message at a time. Come to the messages with an open heart and awareness of all that lies there.

I encourage you to read a paragraph at a time, and then to sit with the vibration until you feel the true meaning of what is being said. Allow that vibration to create a new way of being for you. Allow it to create a new understanding, and a bigger picture than what you normally envision.

Included with this "Show Me" book is a free meditation download kit. You will find the download link following the meditations. These meditations are yours to use whenever you need a reconnection to Spirit and your higher self.

If you are reading the meditations, I suggest you find a quiet place where you can be undistracted. Begin by reading through the meditation, then follow the directions provided. Be sure to set the book aside and pause or listen to music for the length of time indicated in each meditation to receive the full benefit.

All words carry a message, and every message has a vibrational component. The purpose is to find the best vibration in your busy life. We are human beings, and we have forgotten about the vibration of what being means. It is the energy and the vibrational component of the words that will help you find your way.

Be still and feel the message, and most importantly, simply enjoy!

Show Me
Why Am I Here?

You are here to teach Love! Plain and simple.

We giggle as we give you this answer, as teaching Love is no simple or easy purpose. You have taken on this purpose because of the depth of your compassion and your love of the human being. You desire to show others how beneficial it is to live in a society of "love polarities" instead of love-hate polarities.

The one hardship of this purpose, for you Angela and for many like you, is the depth of compassion you possess. The depth and vastness of your compassion may stand in the way of teaching the love polarities — meaning you may just allow your compassion to override your willingness and ability to teach. Compassion does not have the same definition for all, and for you, Angela, compassion has a fine line.

This can become a problem when your love desires to take away another person's experience because of the level of pain and suffering you perceive. When compassion turns into sympathy, you will find yourself trying to help too much. Your healing mind and soul become overwhelmed by witnessing other's suffering, and through this witnessing you create much pain and suffering for yourself. When you are not able to express the vibration of love you desire to match your true emotion, your compassion becomes a force of healing energy, which sometimes heals when it should allow others to heal themselves. Be patient, Angela!

You must remember the laws of free will and the dynamics of human beings wanting to keep their sovereignty and maintain their view of polarity for this world and the galaxies. The point will be to plant the seed of love polarities within the thought system, finding joy in life and living out a life of joy rather than constantly searching for the next best thing to come along.

This is not a judgment; rather, it is an alternative to pain and suffering. The theory of pain and suffering has served its purposes on the earthly plane, but now life in the human form needs to change, grow, and expand. To take on this enormous task is very impressive, and you volunteered. So, now, go forth and teach!

Remember your power
through self-love.

Show Me Who Am I?

You are a simple ray of light existing in the vastness of all the galaxies. You change, fluxing in and out with every breath you take. You create vibrations of love, which have the ability to change color and to heal others and yourself. You create vibrations of light to explore and play with in your life.

Most importantly, you are Love. You are nothing more and nothing less than rays of loving energy. You have the ability to create rays of love everywhere and anywhere, spreading intentions of love and healing. You are constantly creating new vibrations of love and new forms of vibrations to spread loving energy to everything and everyone. You have the ability to visualize this creation of loving vibrations as writing codes or changing codes to streamline life for your fellow human beings.

The vastness of my Love for you is so great that it cannot be confined. Nor can it be bridled. Try to imagine galaxies upon galaxies upon galaxies: that is where you can start to feel the vast energy of your Love. Imagine your loving vibration being so strong that the sun has to protect itself by the moon to keep from burning up. It is also so compassionate that it holds itself back so it does not upset the current flow of the universes.

In one moment of time you are a ray of pink vibration, then changing and growing into a ray of yellow, changing and transforming as your awareness moves through the universe. Then, you become a ray of blood red; then black, transmuting, healing, and creating new love patterns and spreading them through all the wondrousness of the galaxies. This energy is so beautiful that the human mind cannot comprehend it. It can only be felt.

This is a love so great that sometimes you wonder if you were to completely let go whether it would destroy this planet on which you live. You hold back! You are not afraid for yourself, but you are afraid for others. Somehow you need to teach others how to love with such force that nothing stands in the way. You are a teacher who wants others to remember their truth and not to be afraid to unleash this vastness of love.

This love you know as God / Universe / Spirit. It is a love so strong, yet filled with much Grace. This love you have is capable of destruction, yet it cannot comprehend destruction. It is a love so compassionate that it allows the most delicate of things to flourish.

I am love!

You are love!

Tell me you can feel it!

Allow your soul to soak it in. Allow the tears to flow as your body trembles with its power. Allow the trembling to clear and heal your wounds, as Love is the power to heal!

Look beyond your physical being to the soul, where your beauty resides within, this is where you find who you are: LOVE.

You are love!
You are love so strong, you are capable of destruction. Yet, your love does not comprehend it.

Show Me Who Can I Be?

As a brilliant ray of light and Love, there is no limit to the abundance I wish for you. Only you put limits on *who* you can truly be. When you ask this question, I send you more energy and love to bust any blocks that your mind holds.

There are no limits to who you can be!

I know you are thinking in terms of this third-dimensional world in which you live, but I encourage you — no, *challenge* you — to go beyond the 3D, beyond this dimension of Earth. Expand your mind. Envision yourself as an organism from another galaxy. Maybe you choose to be dust from a star. Or maybe, just maybe, you choose to be a ray of colored love that lights the path for a fellow soul.

You see, when you think in 3D, you remain in your third-dimensional, physical world. I want you to expand to the far reaches of infinite possibilities, where everything is always possible. Where everything is *expected* to be a miracle within a miracle, where there is no limit to your brilliance.

You see, you can be anything and everything your soul desires. The possibilities are limitless. The mind is only a small piece of who you really can be. Look within to find the more expansive version of you.

When you look within what do you see?

What do you hear?

Most importantly, what do you feel?

When you allow yourself to feel who you can be, you stand in your own power to be anything and everything. Create something new — something no one has seen or heard before. Then and only then do you know who you can be. When you look within, I will show you. I will help you.

Come, look within and be expansive! Be the unlimited grace of who you are meant to be. Be Love that transcends the limit of the mind.

Create everything, and create nothing.

The options are yours to be!

Words cannot begin to describe
the vastness of my love.

A Meditation on Creativity

Before you begin your meditation you may find it helpful to record this written meditation in your own voice on a recording device. You may also download the complimentary Show Me Meditation Kit using the links below. Then, find a comfortable place to sit in your home or office, play your favorite music or listen to nature sounds. Get comfortable and allow yourself to expand.

FREE DOWNLOAD: To download your complimentary *Show Me Meditation Kit*, go to http://angelablaha.com/book-meditation-downloads/ or scan the QR code.

BEGIN BY SITTING QUIETLY, allowing your body to relax, releasing the weight of the world to the earth to transform and heal as it needs to. Close your eyes, take in a deep breath, and then release that breath. Relax your head and shoulders, and continue to take deep belly breaths to release any stress and tension that has built up in your body. Move your awareness to your chest and arms, relaxing them. Continue to breathe and with each breath allow all stress or tension to be released. With each breath, allow the belly, hips, and legs to relax as well.

Bring your focus and attention to the breath, feeling the coolness of the breath as it enters the nose and the warmth as it exits the nose. Just allow the mind, body, and spirit to relax. Breathe at your normal pace and allow your imagination to expand.

With every breath, allow yourself to feel lighter, gently allowing your physical body to be weightless and relaxed. Allow your mind to relinquish any thought. Imagine each thought simply floating toward the stars. You are simply being at peace.

It is safe to expand to the outer reaches of the earth or galaxy. You are floating freely, enjoy being in the peace that other dimensions allow. Simply imagine, allowing your mind to expand as far as it feels safe to do so. Allow yourself to create new thoughts, new words, new actions. Allow your imagination to create what ever it desires.

5 to 10 minutes of expansion*

Now, let's begin to bring ourselves back into this world. Come back to this time and space, back to this room you are sitting in. Take a deep breath, and move back into your body at this moment in time.

Move your fingers and toes, wrists, and ankles. Take another deep breath. Then, when you are ready, open your eyes.

---

* Be with the silence or listen to your favorite music. Be sure to take the full amount of the recommended time for maximum benefit.

Show Me What Is Important for Me to Know Today?

Today I sit on the steps on the back of my home, I begin to open my channel to Archangel Metatron as I begin my daily writings. As I sit here, I gaze upon the sun on the horizon, and my day begins. I hear the sun ask, "How did you wake?"

I contemplate this question and wonder: did I wake in a good mood? Or did the alarm clock stir me from a deep and pleasant dream?

This is important, because it sets the tone for your entire day. When you wake, review the mind. Simply check in to see what is happening. Do not judge any awareness that you notice. Simply be aware.

If waking is difficult for you, immediately ask for your team or angels to help with the morning rise. Set an intention before you go to sleep at night to arise with pleasure, feeling completely rested, eager to see what new adventures await the new dawn.

It is easy to bring self-love to your reality, and it begins with the moment you open your eyes in the morning. Tonight, before you lay your head to rest, set your intention. You may wish to take a moment to write down your intention now.

Let this intention be the first thing your eyes gaze upon as you wake. It only takes a moment of time, and this practice can bring so much joy into your life.

With my first awakened moment, there will be peace, love, and joy in my thoughts. I will feel this peace, love, and joy as a current running through my body.

I love who I am!

My body, mind, and soul will create a glorious magical balance, bringing more joy to every moment of this special day. And so it is!

Show Me What Are Vibrations?

Vibrations! We would love if you wrote your experience of what vibrations feel like to you, Angela. Vibrations are an important part of life, even though this is not a topic you typically focus on in the course of your human journey. Words, actions, thoughts, and emotions each have a vibration to them, which can bring peace or disturbance to your being.

Angela: As I sit in nature on this beautiful and unseasonably warm morning, I begin to notice a quiet vibration of awakening. The pheasants begin to cackle as they fly from their roosting place in the tree grove to the dam where fresh water awaits. Their cackling vibration rings in my ears, sending a vibration of wild nature cascading through my body.

Nearby, a few remaining birds sing their songs of praise as the earth warms. The sun's vibration begins to warm my home as the wood within the walls begins to crack with the sounds of settling into the day.

My body begins to warm, and I give thanks! I pay attention to the warming vibration, which in turn sends chills down my spine. As this warming vibration continues to pulse through me, I feel peace and a sense that all is as it should be with the world in this moment of time.

When I move my attention to the sound of passing vehicles on the nearby highway, I notice their vibrations of hurry. Rushing here and there, the traffic creates a nervous vibration that moves the earth beneath me as I allow it to penetrate the souls of my feet.

As I look across the landscape, I witness change. The grass is now brown. The leaves have fallen, creating bareness in the landscape. My awareness of the constant, though ever-changing vibration, seems to offer an alert to all my senses as if to tell me soon I will experience something different from what I am now experiencing. There is no wind this morning, which brings an extra vibration of peace from the plants and trees, a certain level of calm felt on the surface of my skin.

A horn honks, disrupting my peacefulness, as if to tell me to move into doing something else. Instead, I long to remain in this peaceful vibration that Mother Earth has brought into my awareness. Then the ego steps in and reminds me of the list of chores that await my attention. My heart replies, "Just a few more minutes — just a few more."

I choose to take a few moments to show the self how much I appreciate and love it before the chaos takes over. I allow the body, mind, and soul to experience the resetting of balance with the world.

I give thanks!

Love is a vibration
that has so many dimensions
that it covers all the universes,
known and unknown.

Show Me

Why Does It Matter That I Love Myself?

Hmmm… Why does it matter? *Why doesn't it matter?* Have you forgotten why you chose to come to Earth?

You chose to come here for the soul purpose of remembering your Love. You chose to come here to experience another kind of Love, a unique perspective. That's all Earth is; it is another form of Love. For the majority of human beings living on Earth, life exists in a cycle of going to work, coming home, eating, praying, getting up, and doing the same thing all over again. We beg you to revisit this perspective as you consider your life.

Being a human and living on Earth is an experience of Love, merely another form of God / Universe / Spirit. This kind of love has many, many layers of vibrations. You see, Earth's expanded form of love is the only one of its kind.

Being on Earth can be very hard. It can be hard emotionally, physically, mentally, and spiritually. The reason your experience is difficult is due to the illusion of separation. The difficulty is caused not by the separation from God / Universe / Spirit or even by your separation from other human beings who share your journey. Rather, it is your separation from yourself that is the origin of pain. The separation of remembering that you are simply Love.

You are layered, expansive, and multidimensional beings with multidimensional expansions or versions of the vibration of love. These layers or expansions have vast ranges to them. You call them polars. You often see these as opposites; rather, we would suggest you choose to think of yourself as existing in dimensional vibrations—an expanded version of a love polarity, a version which you see as opposites. We offer that this version does not have to have opposites.

When we talk about layers or expansions, we want you to think in terms of vibrations. Think about sound waves, and try to envision your vibration in this manner, as expanded frequencies of love. When you hear a bell chime, there are many different sounds or vibrations that emanate from that one chime.

We want you to start thinking and experiencing love in those penetrating sounds or vibrations—feelings of love communicated in a range of multidimensional vibrations. Imagine a vibration so expansive that you cannot witness any end to that vibration. This expanded version of you is how we want you to envision the love you are.

Let's think for a moment about the loving relationships in your life. Begin first by imagining a spouse, partner, or significant other. Think about all the different kinds of interactions you have with this one person throughout the course of a single day. What if you saw each of those interactions as vibrations? Imagine those interactions as bell sounds. As you do, notice that some are deep and resonant, while others are lighter with a higher pitch.

Now, imagine the vibrations coming from those intermingling sounds. How do they feel within your body, your mind, and your soul? Where do you feel them? Do some penetrate at a deeper level than others? We want you to resonate with all your bodies — physical, mental, emotional, and spiritual — not just one or the other. When we talk about all your bodies, we are talking about your physical body, your mental body (the brain), your emotional body, and your spiritual body.

You work as a whole unit; therefore, it is important to bring all your bodies together to more clearly understand why it is important to love yourself. Your emotions are not separate from your soul, nor are they separate from the physical body.

When we bring all the bodies into one, it changes everything. The mind works with the ego, and the ego works with the emotions. Your emotions, in turn, work with the soul. All of these reside within the physical body, creating a whole, multi-dimensional, multi-expansive, and multi-vibrational human being. You are not separate from your parts. *You are one!*

So, let's return to why it matters that you love who you are. When you chose to come to Earth to experience this expansive love, your soul took on a significant challenge. You agreed to come here to be as one with all your bodies and to create a wholeness that cannot be experienced from any other world, universe, or galaxy.

It is very important that the soul learns to embody all of its parts, so that it may experience this form of love on its earthly journey. Choosing to come to Earth for this expansive experience of love may be a once in a soul-time experience. Or the soul may choose to experience it time and time again.

When the soul learns and experiences all of its parts as a whole, the soul's journey is one step closer to enlightenment. In the same way, every soulful experience leads you one step closer to expansion, and expansion is continuous, never ending. So, allow your soul to experience the many different vibrations of love.

This part of your soul's journey is very important. It is a part of the journey that can take many lifetimes to accomplish if that is what you choose.

Expand your mind, your soul, and your heart. Embrace your emotions. Embrace your spiritual body. Connect with all your bodies, and understand that what affects one part affects the whole.

When you allow yourself to feel emotional hurt, it affects your whole self. The hurt affects your emotional body. The hurt affects your spiritual body. The hurt affects the mental / thinking / ego body, and the hurt also affects the physical body.

Stop telling yourself not to feel. Stop numbing yourself with your distraction of choice. Start living in all your bodies. There is no easy way to do this. The only way is to work through it. There is no easy out. There are, however, plenty of do-overs.

You actually need to do this work in order to accomplish what you came here for. You came here to feel the multiple layers of love. In order to feel those many rich layers, you need to do the work, expand, and enjoy the ride.

Change your perspective from negative to positive. Love every ounce of how, what, and who you are. If you don't like something you do or say, change it! You have free will to be the human being you choose to be.

Is it important that you love who you are? Yes, it is vitally important. It is important, because without self-love it is more difficult to embrace the self as a whole. Without self-love, you live in the opposite of that. We do not want you to live your life without knowing and loving who you are at your core.

You are one person, one mind, one spirit. You are not separate from any part of who you are. So, embrace the gift you are, and love YOU!

Paint the air with your love.
Make it indescribable.

Show Me What Is the First Step in Loving Myself?

The fist step in loving yourself is to be kind to you. Do you treat yourself as well as you treat other people? You should be treating yourself much more tenderly, without judgment and with more compassion than you do anyone else!

If you need an another step, let it be forgiveness. Forgiveness is not about forgiving someone else for what they have done to you or said to you. Rather, forgiveness is about you. The most important person involved is you. Now that may sound egotistical, but it really isn't. Let us explain.

When we forgive ourselves for taking on someone else's emotions, that is true forgiveness. When we forgive ourselves for judging our own action or someone else's action, that is forgiveness. When we forgive ourselves for feeling a certain way toward ourselves or toward someone else, that, too, is forgiveness.

When Angela was younger, she was taught to forgive others. Really, she should have been taught to forgive herself for feeling a certain way, acting a certain way, or speaking a certain way. It would have served her well to have been shown how to forgive herself for taking on someone else's emotions or judging herself too harshly.

Forgiveness is for the self. We cannot express how important this point is.

When we forgive ourselves, we heal emotional wounds. These emotions may have just been created. Or they could be attached to a past memory, which is ignited by a current action, word, or thought. When we forgive ourselves, it changes our perception, because we no longer carry that wound with us. When we heal wounds, we heal our current life-time as well as past and future lifetimes. When we forgive ourselves, we allow love to enter us, creating a more expansive version of the self.

So, the next time you get into an argument with someone, forgive yourself for speaking in a way that is not the true representation of who you are. Instead, view it as an emo-tional representation that was allowed to spin out of control. Forgive yourself for using harsh or punishing words. Forgive yourself for being hurt or for feeling guilt and shame. Forgive yourself for not standing in your powerful, true self — the self that loves so much that sometimes we cannot help ourselves or stop our deep desire to fix everyone or everything as we see fit.

The next time you look in the mirror, say, "I love me!" Speak these words without judging the bags under your eyes or the way your hair looks. Say them without bringing your attention to the fact that you are ten pounds under your ideal weight or otherwise disparaging your shape and form.

The next time someone walks through the door to your office and you can feel how upset they are, allow them to be. Do not rush over and try to fix them. They cannot be saved or fixed. We can only save ourselves, and we do that through love and, if needed, through forgiveness of the self.

What Is the First Step in Loving Myself?

The next time someone chooses to transition from their earthly form, love them so much that you allow them to go. Do not hold onto them, creating pain and suffering for yourself through guilt or loneliness. Instead, feel them around you. Trust that they hear your every word. Forgive yourself for being lonely; heal that part of you that desires them to come back in the physical form, and love who you are.

No one has the power to give you the love for which you are searching. That kind of love comes only from within you, not from outside of you. It is the love that you came to Earth to experience and to be.

The next time you forget to do something, forgive yourself. The next time someone calls you a name, do not allow yourself to get hurt or to get angry, instead forgive your-self for not standing in your power of love. Acknowledge them for teaching you a valuable lesson. Understand that such a scenario happens not because you are weak; instead, it may be possible that you are unaware of your power.

Remember that everything we do, everything we say, and every action we take is our responsibility. You chose your reaction. Choose wisely, dear friends. Choose what is a true representation of the love you have inside. Choose how you want to be known.

Do you wish to be known for love and kindness or something else?

We are used to dealing with our shortcomings. We know how to emotionally handle our perceived failures.

I ask you, "What about your love? Do you know how to handle your love?"

Show Me How Can I Remember What Divine Love Is?

You will need to use your imagination for this one!

Put yourself in the most calm, peaceful place you have ever been on Earth. Go ahead, do it. Then magnify that by a million. Now, add love — real, unconditional love. Then, magnify that by a million again. Sit in the sun and feel the warmth and pleasure of the sun. Magnify that by a million.

Now, move to your bed where you can become so comfy that you want to stay there all day long. Wrap up this feeling, as if you are wrapping it up in a warm blanket taken fresh from the sun-kissed clothesline doused in the smell of a beautiful, warm Spring day. This is an ounce of the feeling you receive from divine love.

Divine Love is powerful. It is so vast that there are not words to describe it. It is only a vibration that is felt at such a deep, experiential level that it cannot be described with language. You have experienced this feeling before, so it will be easy to remember your Divine Love.

In your next meditation, ask God / Universe / Sprit to allow you to witness divine love just for a moment. All you need is a moment to feel the expansive vibration of who you are. This vibration of love is kind and gentle, yet also strong and pure. Use the meditation that follows to help with this remembering.

Love is the word to describe a feeling that really has no words.

A Meditation on Divine Love

Before you begin your meditation you may find it helpful to record this written meditation in your own voice on your computer or recording device. Or you may download the complimentary Show Me Meditation Kit using the links below. Then, find a comfortable place to sit in your home or office, play your favorite music or listen to nature sounds. Get comfortable and allow yourself to expand.

 **FREE DOWNLOAD:** To download your complimentary *Show Me Meditation Kit*, go to http://angelablaha.com/book-meditation-downloads/ or scan the QR code.

PLEASE CLOSE YOUR EYES and take in a deep, relaxing breath and acknowledge your life force. Let's begin by relaxing the body, mind, and spirit. Begin with a few deep belly breaths, releasing any stress or tension. Simply allow that tension to fall to the earth to be transposed, transmuted, and healed.

Bring your awareness to the crown of your head, relaxing every muscle at the scalp, moving your awareness from your crown and relaxing your face and neck. Continue to breathe normally and release the shoulders, allowing your shoulders to fall down and away from your head. Now bring your awareness to your arms and allow them to hang free or to rest in your lap. Continue moving your awareness to your chest, belly, and hips, release and relax your muscles there. Allow the legs to release and relax as well.

Allow your body to be still, to be at ease, taking in deep, penetrating breaths that fill the belly with life force energy. Allow all your cells to open, creating a vast, open body of energy, vibrating at warp speed.

Allow the mind to release any thought. Now bring your awareness to your heart center. Open your soul with a deep breath in, allowing yourself to expand to your outer limits of your being. You are safe in your love.

Be still and ask your spirit to allow the feeling of your divine love to be present in your soul. The love of bliss and grace. Allow your love to fill your entire body and mind, feeling joy and happiness with the remembrance of unconditional love.

Enjoy 5 to 10 minutes of expansion through silent meditation

Remembering this vibration is easy. It comes naturally for you. Bring it into your everyday life and allow it to fill you with divinity, compassion, and love.

Bring your awareness back into the room you are in. Bring your awareness back to your body. When you are ready, you can begin to wiggle your fingers and toes. When you are ready, open your eyes.

Show Me

How Can I Learn to Be Enough?

Are you ever enough? Does enough have an ending?

The soul has no ending. With that being said, it is unclear to us that you would desire to ever be enough! Even being in a state of enlightenment is a form of expansion, an ever-evolving notion, continuously expanding into something more. The soul never ends. It is always in a state of change, creating, loving, and experiencing.

There are no souls who are ever enough. Even God / Universe / Spirit is in a continuous pattern of change and flow. As long as there is life in one form or another, there will never be enough of anything, as there is no end. What would life be if we decided to be enough? We would stop growing, changing, and expanding. We would cease to exist.

We are creative beings who create. To be enough would mean the end of creating and, thus, the end of being. We are not ready for the end of creation or the end of being. There is much work to be done before we call it quits! There are many layers of vibration that have not yet been experienced.

How can we ever be enough?

Another answer to your question would be this: when we all remember we are only love, we cease searching because we become "enough" to be satisfied here on Earth. When you remember love so brilliantly that it almost hurts, then and only then will you ever feel as if you are somewhat enough.

But then you will become intrigued with something else, and the search starts all over again. At the end of one destination, another begins.

For example, consider the multitude of layers of love here on Earth. There are so many multidimensional love vibrations that it is hard to get or feel enough of just one of those expansive layers. Not to mention experiencing the range or depth of these layers.

Even in grief, sadness, frustration, guilt, and shame, there are layers of love. Everything comes from love. Even the words and feelings you view as negative. They are simply different vibrations of love. They are part of the dimensional world of Earth. Everything is simply a part of the whole, just as you are a part of the whole.

We encourage you to review your perception and the meaning you have attached to the word "enough". Take it completely out of your vocabulary. Change your perception. Ask instead:

What can I experience today?

What layer or expansion or vibration of love can I feel today?

You are never enough; yet, you are always enough. This may be confusing, but if you allow your mind to expand and see Earth as a part of your universe, your universe as a part of your galaxy, and your galaxy as a part of other galaxies and then even further galaxies, you see there is no end.

There is only more. Yet, every part is enough as it is within itself and within which it is. You are enough as you are. Yet, are you ever done being enough?

Love is the heart's pace
as you gaze into your soul
through your eyes.

Show Me
How Can I Cultivate Authenticity?

We cultivate our authentic self by learning all we can about who, what, how, and why we are the way we have chosen to be. It is a learning experience that is ever changing and evolving.

Your authentic self is not the same self as it was when you were five years old, and it will not be the same when you are 85 years old. Remember that you are energy, and energy is forever changing. So, we invite you to constantly ask "Who am I?" and live the answer you receive, because the answer you receive is always given by your higher self. Who you are is not a fixed answer; rather, it is forever changing.

You made many decisions and created an infinite number of timelines about who you are before your soul came into this lifetime. Your timelines are created depending upon the choices you make in life. Your timelines create your infinite ability to grow and change as you need or desire, all the while creating and updating your authentic self.

Cultivating your authenticity is not a once-in-a-lifetime event, done and then forgotten. Instead, it is a moment-to-moment decision, and one decision can create numerous possibilities. You choose all the parts and all the events that determine how that will look in your life.

Life is so exciting!

Can you imagine what life would be like if we did not get to choose? Every aspect of who you are is chosen by you. From the way we look to how we act to what we want to remember. It is all up to you. There are so many life-altering events, and we choose all of them.

So, continue to grow and expand each and every day. There is no end to cultivating your authenticity. And YOU are the one that chooses everything through your amazing free will.

We will say that the more you know yourself, your real soul self, the easier it is to make decisions based on how you planned this life to be for you. When we become hyperaware of the self, life flows easily. Decisions are then made by asking the soul for advice and following through according to our soul's plan instead of the ego's interpretation of that plan.

Here are a few simply steps to get you started:

1. **Be hyperaware of everything**, especially of what works well for you and what does not. If working for someone else makes you frequently angry or you become frustrated with how the company operates, ask yourself why? What is it I need to learn? What do I need to do to be in flow with my purpose?

2. **Take action steps** to make your wants, dreams, and desires a reality. Only you can make your life happen!

3. **Be in a state of openness**, always knowing that you are able and ready to change when you need or desire to.

How Can I Cultivate Authenticity?

Start with knowing there is no end to being your authentic self. You are a changing being all the time. Be all you can be by growing and expanding constantly. Do not be afraid of change. Change can set you free.

Love is a vibration
that holds energy together.

Show Me What Does It Mean to Be Compassionate?

Ah… compassion!

This may be one of the most difficult of vibrations and most complex of the emotions, because compassion is two-fold. It can be a more layered vibration than love as it can lure the heart to help others no matter their situation, which in essence adds to the vibration of compassion, making it feel even deeper and more vast than it actually is.

You may feel so compassionate toward someone or about something that it creates a passion. In such times, there is no stopping its momentum. We are not suggesting that it is bad to be compassionate or to feel compassion. It is good to have compassion. However, when compassion has no boundaries, it may go overboard.

Let's look at Angela's compassion to help and heal others. She shows people a tough exterior sometimes, because that is her way of protecting her very compassionate, loving heart. Sometimes her compassion and her desire to heal someone can go overboard. In such situations, instead of healing, she may inadvertently cause more pain and suffering — not for others but for herself.

She can sometimes be so compassionate that she takes on someone else's problem or tries to heal someone without allowing them the space to work through their own emotions. Being this compassionate may leave the person she is trying to help in a difficult place as they have not learned their own lessons through the experience of creating their own healing.

When we take someone else's lesson or experience on and make it our own, they do not get to experience the healing of the emotional wound. This is something their soul may have a great yearning to experience. When we take on someone else's experience, we rob them of the opportunity to have this experience for themselves. Some experiences may be perceived as dark or very harmful; however, that is a judgment and should be left to the discretion of its creator.

So you see how compassion is excellent to have but requires delicate balance and understanding. We find it quite amazing how people have all these emotions, yet their understanding and control of those emotions is very limited.

Learn to understand how compassion feels for you. When you have the sense of feeling compassionate toward another person or toward something in your environment, ask yourself:

Is this compassion?

It is love?

Is it something else?

Rarely do you feel only one emotion at a time. Emotions are generally combined, which makes it even more difficult to distinguish what it is you are truly feeling or experiencing.

What Does It Mean to Be Compassionate?

For this reason it is imperative that you learn all about you. Learn all about your emotional body. Learn all about your spiritual body. Learn all about your mental body and your physical body.

When you know yourself inside and out, then you can make sound decisions based in wisdom and love. Otherwise, you are simply floundering and flopping around, starving for breath like a dying fish.

The more you grow and expand, the easier it is to understand all parts of yourself and the emotions that arise. The more you understand, the easier it is to feel all your parts. When you put them all together, you allow wisdom and love to flow through your life.

To be compassionate is to love so much that you allow everything and everyone to be in their own dimension of evolution. It is an act of compassion to care about someone or something and to help and serve when you can, but do not take anything, any lesson, or any feeling away from those who seek your help. To be compassionate allows you to give, to teach others to stand in their power of love, and to show love and healing, but never take love or healing away from another.

To be compassionate is to be kind, yet strong. It is to be empathic, yet encouraging. To be compassionate is to show others how to be courageous as you stand in your own power of unconditional love and teach others to do the same. To teach others to stand in their own strength and to allow them to be where they choose to be: this is true compassion.

I am vulnerable and afraid, yet so powerful. I am worthy and filled with love.

Show Me What Does It Mean to Be Vulnerable?

Being vulnerable is not a bad thing. We just want you to know that being vulnerable opens up so many doorways to possibilities. Being vulnerable is one of the quickest ways to expand and grow, and it is perfectly divine to allow yourself to be vulnerable.

Being vulnerable offers proof to yourself that change needs to happen in order for you to grow and expand to your fullest capacity. When we are vulnerable, we do not necessarily open ourselves up for attack or harm, although that can happen if we live a fearful life.

When we live in fear, being vulnerable has a very different meaning. According to the online version of Merriam-Webster dictionary:

> **Vulnerable:** *easily hurt or harmed physically, mentally, or emotionally; open to attack, harm, or damage.*

When we come from a fear-based mentality, attack physically, mentally or emotionally is very possible, because we are coming from a place of believing that such an attack can happen. When we believe something can happen, it inevitably will happen sooner or later, relating in part to the Law of Attraction. What you think will happen, will. It is a form of self-sabotage to live from a place of fear.

The definition above can be quite frightening, but the meaning itself is rooted in fear. There is a definite polarity to the meaning, and we ask you to be discerning in your understanding of vulnerability.

When we come from a place of love, experiencing vulnerability can simply indicate that change is happening. In such times, we open ourselves up to infinite possibilities. When we open ourselves to these possibilities, we rid ourselves of the rules about what those possibilities look like. We shed our preconceived perceptions of how such change will occur and the potential outcomes of those many possibilities.

Being vulnerable can be a beautiful emotional, physical, or mental experience when we create a positive intent and leave ourselves open to our highest potential, eliminating a negative experience by our positive intent. You see, every emotional experience, every physical experience, every spiritual experience, and every mental experience can have a polarity within it.

Everything has a flip side, because we live in a world where polarities are strong. So, depending upon whether you come from fear or from love, your outcome is based in a positive or a negative experience. We suggest you choose to come from a place of love. In doing so, being vulnerable will mean an openness to possibilities with multidimensional experiences.

What Does It Mean to Be Vulnerable?

By being vulnerable we open the door to infinite possibilities.

Show Me

How Can I Experience My Power?

Power is a tricky word!

The ego loves the word power. It has a way of turning the word *power* into a very strong emotion which can create a "rise above" or become mentally "better than" attitude. We would love for you to acknowledge your own power by *being* love. That is what you are: Love, in all forms.

When we talk about power — *your* power — it is with respect for who, what, how, and where you are on your soul's journey. There is a certain amount of understanding, wisdom, and creation in the vibration of the word *power*. We would offer that you connect with these traits or vibration of the word and see if it matches your definition.

There is an equal word to *power*, and that is *love*. If you want to know your power, as we said before, you will know it through the many different forms of love. For us, love is your power. When you stand in your power, you stand in your love, your truth. The vastness and openness to love yourself as well as everything in the earthly world and outside the earth is a very powerful position to be in.

When you stand in your power, you speak your truth, you know you are authentic, and you are not afraid to be who you are. We love this about you!

To experience your power we offer a meditation for your enjoyment.

How Can I Experience My Power?

Stretch beyond the mind and spirit into unchartered territory.

A Meditation on Personal Power

Before you begin your meditation you may find it helpful to record this written meditation in your own voice on your computer or recording device. Or you may download the complimentary Show Me Meditation Kit using the links below. Then, find a comfortable place to sit in your home or office, play your favorite music or listen to nature sounds. Get comfortable and allow yourself to expand.

 **FREE DOWNLOAD:** To download your complimentary *Show Me Meditation Kit*, go to http://angelablaha.com/book-meditation-downloads/ or scan the QR code.

RELAX THE BODY by taking in a deep breath, allowing the jaw to drop and the shoulders to relax. Close your eyes and bring your awareness to the rest of your body, beginning with your head and work all the way down to your toes. Relax each muscle, so the body is completely at ease.

Breathe slowly and allow your body to relax. Bring all of your attention to your heart — that place where your soul resides within the body.

Now, think of a place where you feel so safe the world could shatter around you, and you would not know of its existence or loss. Get so comfortable that nothing else matters. Breathe into this safe place, creating a feeling of comfort, grace, and joy.

Allow your mind to open. Allow your heart to open. Expect nothing. Just be in the safety of the feeling of love in all forms. Allow love in all forms to enter into your mind and into your heart.

Breathe in. Breathe out. Allowing your body to be at ease. Allow your mind to open to the feeling of unconditional love in all forms. Allow your body to open to unconditional love in all forms. Allow your heart to open to unconditional love in all forms.

Allow unconditional love in all forms to enter and to be felt within your soul. Allow your soul to remember this feeling. Simply allowing. Give yourself this gift of remembering. You are safe in your unconditional love.

Enjoy 15 minutes of music

Now, give thanks to yourself for allowing the freedom of remembering. Give thanks to your soul, you mind, and your body. Give thanks to the love energy.

Take a deep breath and come back into the body, bringing your awareness back into the self. Now you have felt your power – the power of love in all your forms.

Be of this love vibration and the feeling it brings to you. Radiate this feeling to the world. Bring it to your everyday life, and be powerful with love.

Heal with the power of Love, create with the power of Love, and be the power of Love.

Show Me What Else Is There to Know about My Power?

We are talking about a word that has so many levels, so many experiences, and so many meanings. Power can be a dangerous word. With that being said, we will speak of power that comes from love only.

Power = Love!

You have the power to create everything in your world. Together you and God / Universe / Spirit created your world, and you are responsible for your life. You have created and continue to create everything in your world!

You create your emotional balance. You create your physical balance. You create your spiritual balance, and you create you mental balance. How? By every choice you make. You are creating your world according to your moment by moment decisions, your free will to choose.

You have the power to change everything in you and around you. You have the power to create love or to create hate. You have the power to save the world or to destroy it. You have the power to come from a place of love with your heart wide open. Or you have the power to come from a place of fear with your heart closed with a narrow perception.

You are power!

You are love!

You are everything!

We want you to know and understand the level of your power. The power of your love resides within you, it is not outside of you. No one holds power or love over you. The level of your power is within the limits of the box you have created around you, often to keep you feeling safe. This feeling of safety is an illusion as your love power is continuously changing, as love and power are energy and energy is forever changing.

When you stretch the walls of your box, you expand, creating a new level of power and creating a new form of you. When you create a new form of you, your love grows and expands, which in turn creates even more power to create your dreams and desires, your wants, your dharma, and your purpose in life. When you understand your purpose(s) in life, you create even more power within you because your understanding of your experience of expansion matches.

Most of us do not come with just one purpose to achieve in life. We come with many purposes, and we create new purposes with every choice we make. When we are finished with one destination, we create another, all the while expanding, evolving, and enlightening to our highest potential in this lifetime.

Be as powerful as you can, but always come from the power of love. Love is what creates. Fear destroys!

What Else Is There to Know about My Power?

Your power is greater than most of you acknowledge or even care to witness. Why? You come from a place of fear, and this fear holds you back from knowing your true authentic self, which is the purest form of love. We encourage you to open to your highest self.

We love you so much, and we hate to witness your pain and suffering, which you create when you come from the mindset of fear. We understand your fear, for unleashing the power of love can be overwhelming at times. We wonder, however, how you are ever going to know what it feels like, looks like, or truly is if you do not allow your walls to crumble around you and awaken to the everlasting feeling of bliss within you?

Once you get a glimpse of the blissfulness, the grace, and the potential to live without fear, it becomes so alluring that you will desire it more and more. It is your birthright to live in bliss! You were never meant to live in the pain and suffering that has become the norm for human beings.

We encourage you to step out of your box and feel the bliss.

Go ahead; take a chance.

Love is easier to experience than fear. Fear create anxiety and stress, making life's decisions difficult and complicated, because you are forever doubting your true ability and your inner wisdom. All love does is create bliss and happiness. When you align with your power of love, life flows, pain and suffering is diminished, and bliss exudes.

When we fill ourselves with love, we are so much more powerful than when we are not filled with love. Love has the power to overcome everything — every obstacle and every action. We want you to understand that power is not brute force. Nor is expressing your power mean you are being cruel or manipulative.

Power is equal to love and should be used to heal, protect, and share. Power is the ability to be born and to die. Power is the ability to live a gracious life in joy and bliss. Power is the ability to love yourself without judgment. Power is the ability to focus on what brings you joy and to live a powerful, joyous life.

Power is being truthful about who you are and who you want to be. Power is the ability to love others without judgment. Power is the ability to be free in the human form that you have chosen.

Power equals love. When we love without conditions, we live in freedom.

Life is a powerful adventure.
Allow your life to skyrocket you
into your divine brightness.

Show Me

Why Is My Energy So Low Today?

Higher Self: This morning when you woke at 5 a.m., the body was cold, creating a wakened state of mind and body. When you decided to remain in bed, hoping you would draw warm blood to pulse throughout your veins and warm the skin, you were creating an illusion. It is important to bring this into your awareness today, Angela.

Angela: I found upon my rolling out of bed that my energy seemed low. Things were agitating my already busy mind. I tried to sit down to meditate and my ever-racing mind did not want to settle into a meditative state of being. I tried to write a "Show Me" message and all I heard was, "Go clean something. You are not ready to write." I laughed to myself. Then, I got up from my chair and started to dust and clean the main floor of my home.

During my frantic pace of cleaning, a friend messaged me. She was testing at the Chopra Center that week and had sent a message expressing how exhausting and difficult the testing was. I remembered being there myself six months earlier. I recalled how stressed I was that whole week and told my friend I would send her some loving energy to help her exhaustive state. Soon she replied, saying she had received the energy and described how "wide awake" she now was.

After that conversation, I finished my cleaning. As the day went on, I realized how exhausted I really was. When I am tired, I do not make good choices and I realized I had not eaten at all, it was already around one o'clock in the afternoon. My solution was to eat a heavy, "dine out" meal loaded with carbohydrates, which, of course, made me even more tired.

It takes a tremendous amount of work for me to maintain this body system, a chore I do not enjoy. Making healthy food choices for this body seems so complex. It seems to take too much energy and require a desire of knowledge I do not care to have, so I eat whatever is quickest, further adding to my exhaustion.

How can I raise my energy and vibration today, in spite of my food choices or the time I got up, I wondered? Self-care feels exhausting and overwhelming at times, even though I know how vitally important it is. As I sit in judgment of my food intake and energy level, I begin to notice my desire and need to slow my mind down. My mind seems to find its own way into a meditative state. I also notice the body following the mind's lead. I sit in awe. I had not noticed this transaction before. I found it quite interesting!

As I sit in silence, my higher self begins to show me pictures of myself. *It all goes back to self love*, I hear. *You know this!* We have discussed this before and you know how to treat yourself with love. What was different about today?

My higher mind reflects on my choices today. When I woke up early from being cold, why did I dismiss getting a blanket for myself? If that had been one of my children or my husband, I would have done it for them. Why not myself?

Why Is My Energy So Low Today?

The mind rests again. As I take a deep breath settling back into the quiet, I hear my soul crying. I take another deep breath to relax even further. Still, the crying grabs my attention. I remain in stillness. My awareness settles into my heart space, from where the sobbing is coming.

A vision comes to my mind from my higher self. I find myself sitting next to my heart as it continues to cry, wondering why I put myself last. Why do I not find it important to put myself at the top along with everyone else? I hear my mind asking why I chose to eat so poorly. It asks why I deemed it necessary to give my energy away when I knew I already felt irritated and somewhat tired. These two things should have been an indication that greater attention to self-care was needed.

My logical mind was taken aback with such clarity around the use of my energy coming into focus. I felt as if I had just received a good tongue-lashing from my mother, although this sharp focus seemed very loving. I paused again to consider the questions that had come into my awareness:

Why do I choose not to put myself at the top of the list?

Do I truly and unconditionally love who I am?

I have been writing about love for days now, yet every action, every word, every thought I have had on this day has not been a reflection of such love. What makes my thoughts, actions, and words different today? After all, I send people loving and healing energy all the time. Why would today be different? I wake up early more often than I care to admit, and food seems to be an ever-present issue for me as I readily see it as a distraction.

So why today? What is different?

"Show me?" I ask. As I go within to an even deeper level of meditation, the physical body complains. My right shoulder aches. My hips begin to scream. My skin is cool, not warm as it usually is.

As I search and ask my emotional, mental, and spiritual bodies, inviting them to show me, I notice I am not surrounded by my spiritual team, the enlightened beings who help guide my higher self. As I bring this into my awareness, I notice the body becomes hot. There is a sense of peace that comes over me, and tears begin to swell in my eyes.

I close my eyes and ask telepathically, in a tone that borders on frantic, "Where are you?" I do not hear an answer. As I gaze lovingly at them in my mind's eye, I find them at last. Their heads are facing downward. Their eyes are closed. My perception deems it necessary to inject a thought of the light beings praying for me. I wonder what is happening.

As I again quiet my mind's chatter and take in a deep breath, I hear, "All is well. We never left. We simply weren't your main focus earlier today. We never leave you. We simply step back when we need to. We can love you from afar as much as we can right next to you. You are never alone! "

"We need to remind you that all your choices are yours to make," they say. "There are no good or bad, right or wrong choices. Instead, view choices as simply different, just as each day is different, as you have witnessed today."

"Lessons are taught in many ways, and today you needed to remember self-love. Try not to get caught up in the hustle of life. Instead, take the few moments of time to care for you. Love yourself, always!" they reply.

I leave my meditative state with more understanding of self-love and the difference it truly makes in my life. I see how the degree to which I love myself influences how I perceive myself and everything around me.

Bring into your awareness
the importance of self-love.

Show Me

How Can I Learn to Expect a Miracle?

Oh sweet soul! Everything is a miracle.

When did it become the norm to not think in miracles?

Every breath you breathe is a miracle. Have you thought about how miraculous the human body is? When you take a breath, it is really a miracle breath, one that you take for granted. As each breath comes into the body, it provides life. Think about that for a moment. Take a deep breath. Witness what happens.

Nutrients are spread throughout the body, mind, and soul with every breath. When we focus on the breath during meditation, it not only calms the body. It also fills and feeds the body. It feeds the mind, creating a pathway to the soul. When we touch the soul, we touch not just one miracle; we open the box to infinite possibilities of miracles.

Every time you speak, think, or eat is a miracle. Living on this beautiful planet Earth is a miracle. Everything is a miracle, and all you have to do is simply change your perception in order to witness miracles and to be a miracle.

Try to envision your whole life as a perspective of learning. View everything as an experience, a miracle. When we come from the viewpoint of experiences, miracles form right before us, because we view life experientially!

When we think in experiences we come from a place of love and creation instead of expectation. When we come from love, we only live in a world of miracles. We encourage you to live in the present moment where miracles happen all the time. Miracles do not happen in the past or in the future. They happen right here, right now, right in front of your eyes.

Miracles are not things that come from heaven. Miracles come from you! You seem to be under the misperception that miracles are experiences that are extraordinary, awesome, fantastic, or out of the normal. Or you see miracles as something being sent from your Creator.

It is *you* that creates miracles, and you are a witness to every miracle you create. Become the master, and view everything in the form of a miracle. That is really all a miracle is: your perception of life, one moment at a time. See your life as the beautiful, miraculous unfolding it is: one miracle after another!

See the miracle you are
as if you are looking through
the eye of Source.

Show Me

How Can I Find Something in Me to Love?

Dearest Soul,

Finding something in you to love should not be as difficult as you are making it to be. Remember that no matter what has happened in your life, what is happening now, or what will happen, you have chosen it to be so. This is very important to remember, because you create every experience you have.

There is no one to blame. Instead, there are experiences to experience and lessons to learn. Your experiences are simply lessons, which your soul has chosen to learn. So we encourage you to ask yourself questions of every situation, every event, every thought, and every action. Ask over and over again:

What am I to learn?

What is it I have chosen to learn in this moment of time?

Stop feeling sorry for yourself or trying to find someone to blame. Your life is neither of those. Rather, your life is an experience after experience with multiple things to learn in each moment of the experience.

When you ask what it is you want to learn, explore all of the possibilities. This can be done by exploring all your bodies as a whole: your emotional body, your physical body, your mental body, and your spiritual body. Become a witness to your experiences.

Explore the emotional body. Emotions often pile on top of each other, so please explore all of the layers of your emotions. Ask:

What emotions am I feeling?

Is there a new emotion to explore?

What is the root emotion?

How can I heal this emotion?

Explore the physical body. The physical body can be an expression of the emotional body. To separate the emotions from the physical, ask:

Where does it hurt?

Is this a pain I have felt before?

Does this pain come into my awareness every time I feel a certain emotion?

How can I stop this pain from occurring or re-occurring?

Explore the mental body. Sometimes our mental body has a hard time with the emotions and our perceptions take over. Explore your truth as you ask:

Why do I perceive this situation this way?

Is this a pattern of thinking that is mine or does it belong to someone else?

How can I change my perception?

Explore the spiritual body. All our experiences happen for a reason. Explore these reasons as you ask:

What have I chosen to learn?

How can I move my soul further on its journey?

Is there something I need to heal or view differently?

These are simple questions to explore in every situation, every thought, and every action. You see, you love yourself so much that you have chosen this life to learn and to experience. You have chosen this life to find new ways to grow on many levels of your expanded self.

There are so many things about you to love that you are overlooking the simple things. Life is not about dramatic events. Rather, life is about simplicity. Life presents us with an opportunity to find awe in everything you do and everything around you.

Simplify your life, and love the way you walk. Love the way your eyes glisten when you feel love. Love the way you smile. Love how you feel when you are in flow with your decisions.

Love the kind gestures you show to your fellow human beings without anyone else noticing. Love the way you notice the rain as it falls to the ground. Love how you wonder what makes it smell so good. Love the way you cry and also the way you pretend you are not crying.

Stop looking for the dramatic "something" to love. Instead, love everything about you, just the way I love you!

Explore the real you!
The you that loves to wonder.
The you that loves to explore.
The you that simply loves.

Show Me How Is Polarity Present in My Life?

We want to talk about polarities. If you choose to continue to live in a world of polarities, we encourage you to think about a Love / Love polarity world rather than a Love / Fear polarity world.

The Love / Fear polarity world has served its purpose and now it is time to expand and evolve. We would love for you consider a Love / Love polarity and all of its many advantages. The vibration of a Love / Love society is very intriguing, wouldn't you agree? Sit back and imagine a Love / Love society for a moment. Feel the vibration of what that would be like in comparison to the vibration of your current society.

Love has many meanings and many forms and levels. Here are just a few:

Compassion	Harmony	Nurture
Intrigue	Like	Reverence
Understanding	Hope	Beauty

Grace	Respect	Authenticity
Purpose	Fondness	Kindness
Cooperation	Ambition	Power
Joy	Collaboration	Charm
Desire	Encouragement	Forgiveness

Each word takes on a different meaning, and each one of you attaches a different perspective to that word, according to how you have understood life to be. None of the meanings are right or wrong. They are simply different, and it is okay to be different.

Love is a tenderness felt by your soul. This love moves throughout your emotional, mental, spiritual and, finally, physical body. Even though love travels throughout all your bodies, humans primarily focus on the physical. This occurs because your physical body is the easiest to experience and understand as it is a visual representation. The physical body alerts you when it feels pain or joy, although this is actually felt as a congruent experience with the emotional, mental, and spiritual body all working as one. When all of our bodies work together, they all feel pain or joy; they do not feel these separate from one another.

We encourage you to experience the tenderness of love within your heart space. Experience it not merely in your physical heart space, but also and especially in your soul's heart space. There exists a euphoric feeling within your soul. We would love for you to explore this feeling further. We acknowledge that this may take some time if you are new to experiencing love in this manner. We encourage you to continue to feel your love in your soul as it will bring you much pleasure.

When we envision and create a Love / Love society, it comes from a place within us that is very deep. It comes from a soul level. How many times are we taught to look within for love? We do live in a world defined by polarity, so why not make the best of this polar perspective by beginning and ending with love?

Love is not cruel,
nor does it think
in cruel terms.

Show Me How Can I Become Shame-Resilient?

Shame is a very emotional word that should not have a part of the human vocabulary.

What is shame? When you were young, were you shamed into behaving in a certain way in accordance with your parent's views or society's rules and expectations? The only way you are taught about shame is from your ancestors. It is passed down from ancestor to ancestor; yet, there is no need to place blame on them, for you took on their understanding of what shame is.

To rid yourself of shame, you need to forgive yourself for carrying it with you. These are old paradigms, old ways of thinking or being, that you took on as your own. You have made these a part of who you are. Forgive yourself for taking on this paradigm. Do not overthink forgiveness or how you took on the blame paradigm. Rather, simply tell yourself that you are now standing in your power of love and will not feel shame from someone else's perspective.

Ask your source to fill you with light and love. Believe and trust that you no longer have or will accept shame into your life. It is really that simple! It is that simple with all old paradigms and old programming. Simply release them, and fill yourself with something joyous and know that it is happening.

We are all energy, and energy changes, transforms, and transmutes itself all the time. The same goes for emotions, feelings, thoughts, and moods. It's all energy! Everything is energy, and energy is in a state of constant change. So now you know how simple it is to change energy. Do not try to make it harder than it really is, as it is very simple to change energy and can easily be done with a change of your perception.

We know you are allowing doubt to enter, possibly wondering about the importance of shame. Shame is a word with a lower vibration. Say the word out loud. What do you feel? When we do something that is not in alignment with our higher self we may feel shame. We would ask that you feel forgiveness, learn from your lesson, and move on.

You see, it is all just a process of believing in something greater than what you are believing in now. As soon as you change your perception and acknowledge everything as energy, everything is possible. Then, everything becomes a miracle, and within each miracle is a field of infinite possibilities. When forgiveness takes over, lessons and experiences are learned and movement once again takes place. You have no limits except the ones you place upon yourself.

Everything is energy and energy is in a state of constant change

Show Me
How Can I Love Myself When I Don't Know Myself?

We would ask in return, why don't you know yourself? It is your job to know what, how, and why you are, as well as who you are. It is your responsibility to live a joyful, happy, and graceful life of love.

When you negate your responsibility to know you are love, then you have created a personal world of self-betrayal. When we succumb to what the world says we should be, instead of being who we are, we create our own pain and suffering.

Begin with loving one aspect of you. Perhaps it is an aspect of your physical body, such as the way you smile. We understand that we have some features that are easier to love than others and since the physical body can be seen it is sometimes easier to begin with the physical appearance. Maybe you love your eyes. Or your hair. Or your creative flair. You see, it really does not matter what you choose. The point is to choose something that you really love about yourself, bring it into your awareness and magnify this beautiful quality you have.

Whatever you choose to bring into focus, bring it into full view, enlarge it, making it larger than life. Love every single color reflected in your eyes, how your eyes are shaped, and how long your lashes are. Maybe you see beyond the physical and love the soul you see when you look deep within your beautiful eyes. Love the way your soul looks back at you when you look into your eyes. *Love it all!*

Then move on to another aspect of you that you unconditionally love. And then another. Keep going until you accept completely and unconditionally love every ounce of who you are.

When you get to the tougher aspects, such as the anger you carry from a childhood memory, you can choose to review the memory, release it to the earth, and know and trust that it is being transformed to a higher vibration. It is this process that allows love to enter, no matter what you used to believe about who you were. You have the power to create you — a power so great it includes love.

If you need more time to heal your wounds, then take all the time you need. Just remember that it is your responsibility to heal your wounds. You created your wounds, and you can heal them through the power of your love. Have confidence in your ability to heal yourself.

We also ask that you do not think too much about knowing yourself or not knowing yourself. Instead, we recommend that you *feel* who you are. Feel the love that is deep within you, accept that love, and allow it to grow. When you feel the love, you stop searching for someone else to make you feel loved, because you understand that only you can bring the love you seek.

Love only comes from within you, and you are perfect as you are.

There is no higher form of love than self-love. When you feel self-love, you feel Source and the power of Source love, because you *are* Source love. Source love is so bright that it conquers and heals all things. When we accept this concept of Source love, it makes knowing the self easy.

Live life in joy,
happiness, and grace.

Show Me Why Is My Life So in Flow Right Now?

Higher Self: There are certain times in your life when everything seems to go perfectly and a feeling of bliss penetrates your every thought, every action, and every word. It is during these times when life simply flows effortlessly, easily, and smoothly. When you are in flow, knowing that you are healing and self-love has entered into your experience, this gives you an understanding that change is here. Angela had one of those times recently and we would like for her to share this experience with you, so you can understand that being in flow can be an everyday occurrence, not just once in a while experience.

Angela: I am sitting in an airport going home from a conference unlike anything I have ever attended before. There were many annoyances during the conference, including many hours wasted on up-selling attendees on new products and services. There were also many "aha" moments that penetrated the mind and soul, allowing a confirmation of how life is so wonderful.

My experience was well worth the few moments of waste according to my perception, because of the many wonderful people I met. Much to my surprise, I made some long-term friendships over the weekend. The people who attended where like-minded people, which I had not expected, as my perception of this conference was that it would simply be a little vacation for me. My perception was clearly off, and I am very grateful I followed my intuitive instinct to attend.

The entire time I was at the conference was effortless. It started the moment I left home, and the feeling of ease and connectedness has continued to this day. This conference was evidence to me that I am on the right path! I enjoy so much the fact that when I listen to my higher self and make choices that create the timelines that assist in my higher learning, life aligns and confirmations are given.

Today, I am at the top of the world in gratitude to myself for having the courage to take steps to be open to and listen to my higher self — the part of myself that is very frank and honest, yet so loving that it is hard to grasp words to describe it. Today I am in flow. Namaste!

Higher Self: Angela's experience was a good choice. She really did not understand why she was being led to this conference. In fact, it really had nothing to do with the conference. Instead, it was time for her to meet some powerful woman who, much like herself, were brought together not because of what they want to do in life but who they want to be. The people she met will be lifelong friends to her, bringing her much needed support.

When you listen to your soul and follow your intuition into the experiences you so desire, good things come. Life is about these fantastic experiences and following the unknown nudges to much deeper experiences that the soul is desiring.

When you are in flow
with your higher self, life flows
easily, effortlessly, and smoothly.

Show Me

Why Is It We Dislike Talking about Self-Love?

We don't talk about self-love because it can sometimes remind us of pain and suffering. Pain comes from many memories of deep wounds that extend from this lifetime or many lifetimes. These wounds have been caused by our perceptions of our action, thoughts, or words, which are compounded by what we have been taught about what is right or wrong, good, or bad.

There is a sense of intense pressure when we think about self-love. This is precisely why we recommend you experience self-love. After all, we are taught not to cry, not to be a wimp, not to show our emotions, not to be afraid (even though we live in a society rooted in fear), and not to give too much. With all of these confinements, why would we want to think about or begin to feel what real self-love is? It will take a whole reprogramming of the mind to allow self-love into our experience. Who has time or even knows where to begin to tackle such a feat?

With these ingrained precepts, we steer away from workshops, books, and practices that attempt to address the subject of unconditional love for ourselves. There is a stereotype of what self-love looks like and feels like, and it seems to be attached to either a type of energy that is thought of as either egotistical or lazy. Neither is an accurate assessment.

Self-love means nothing of the sort. All self-love really means is that YOU unconditionally love yourself, with all your good and not-so-good points. Love yourself as you are and as you desire to be.

Is it really that simple? Yes! It is really that simple.

Angela: I give clients a simple exercise to do to begin the process of allowing themselves to feel and understand self-love. It is called Soul Gazing. You look at yourself in the mirror, look only into the pupil of your eyes. This is where you can see the soul. Not only do you see your soul, but your soul sees you as well. Go ahead, put this book down, and go do it.

What did you see?

Did you experience the love you have inside?

If not, go do it again. Do it until the tears flow down your face. Look deep within until your body trembles with the release of anxiety that you have been carrying for a long time. Look at your soul. See how beautiful you are, and how loving you are. See how peaceful, joyous, and filled with grace you are.

Look, look! Don't be afraid to see the real you. You have spent all these years seeing the fake you, and you have put up with that version of you. Now it is time to see the real, unscripted, beautiful sense of love you are.

Now, make your experience concrete with journaling. Here are a few questions you can use in your writing meditation today:

Why would we hide this feeling?

Why Is It We Dislike Talking about Self-Love?

Why are we programmed not to tap into such divine love that has no judgment?

Why would we deny ourselves this exquisite ability to love so deeply that nothing else in the world matters?

This kind of love does not belong to one group of beings. It does not matter what your economic status is or what cultural group you claim. None of that matters. It belongs to each and every one of us, yet we deny ourselves this profound divine right. It is one of the gifts given to us by God / Universe / Spirit, yet we deny we know anything about it. We deny such an incredible feeling of love that lives within us.

We avoid talking about self-love because of pain and suffering we have experienced. These experiences have emotions attached to our memories, creating an uncomfortable situation.

Show Me What Is the Vibration of a Soul as It Heals?

As tears fill your eyes, allow the feeling of love which is so vast and deep that it is hard to put the emotion into words. Feel the vibration of exuberance from another human being as he or she feels the healing energy of love. This feeling is so expansive it is difficult to explain in words as it is only at a level of vibration. How do you explain a vibration? Words are too limiting to even describe the emotion or even the sense of the emotion when a soul heals with love.

In fact, the word "emotion" itself is limiting. The vastness and depth of the healing sensation of love can be full of excitement, peace, exuberance, and grace.

Have you truly felt someone else's heart when you are in love with them? The heart races, the face flushes, and the eyes soften. There is such a sense of connectedness, the earth could fall from beneath your feet and you wouldn't even care. When eyes meet eyes and souls see each other, there are no words to explain what is completely felt.

Some of you may have a fearful sense that creeps into your existence when you think about the emotion of love. You wonder just how lost the heart can become with this feeling of love, and the thought of losing control is terrifying. All the while, the logical mind is cautioning you of hurt, reminding you of what you witnessed many years ago. This memory still claims its emotion, holding you from any healing or new experience.

You are simultaneously remembering that you perceived the memory to be healed, yet the memory raises an emotion within you that brings discomfort. Your logical mind rationalizes that you should be released from this feeling. Allowing this love to take on an energy of its own is a bit foreign. From some other distant memory you realize you can create a new mental picture with new memories and new emostrings.

> **Emostring:** *a very strong emotional feeling which pulls at your heartstrings.*

Some souls can come into life very wounded, with centuries of hurt, anguish, and pain. Like slashes a starving tiger makes in its prey's flesh, these wounds can be deep. Those wounds can bleed profusely. It can seem as if they will never be healed. They can be so deep, it can seem, if they do heal at all, the scars will surely remain for centuries. These wounds will need pure love to completely heal. Love is the only energy which can heal the soul.

When the soul is healing from such a wound, a vibration of confusion sometimes results. This confusion is created by our logical brain trying to hold onto the comfort of what it knows and understands. The logical brain tries to forgive and to free itself from pain and misery, yet it does not like to change. Allowing the confusion to pass through the bodies can be helpful. Just allow the awareness to pass through all your bodies as if it were floating on a stick that the rushing water carries downstream.

Once the confusion has made its way through, then comes the new

What Is the Vibration of a Soul as It Heals?

vibration of healing. For some of us, this can be a totally new experience. Again, try not to judge. Simply allow it to come in and enjoy the experience of healing.

Allow love to enter, allowing these new feelings to create new emotions, new words, and new experiences. You are not alone, for you have your soul.

You are not alone,
for you have your soul, your love.

Show Me What Is the Root of My Thoughts?

Vibrations! The vibration of love is at the root of thought. When we try to envision what thought is, what do we see?

Do thoughts come from a place that is unknown, from a mysterious place? Or are thoughts simply ideas that suddenly appear out of nowhere? Where do they come from?

We offer this explanation: thoughts come from your mind and soul creating ideas of what you desire or need. They come from your remembrance of the vibration of love and from what you are striving to return to as your soul makes its journey home.

However, love's vibration can be misconstrued. Sometimes, we are unable to find love's true meaning. It can fail to find its true vibration because of overuse or misuse. Love's vibration may be missing in action, afraid to emerge from the dark depths of pain and suffering as it seems to have been stuck in some other emotion than Love.

When fear enters into our notion of what love is, the entire physical, mental, emotional, and spiritual systems take a different direction. Fear is fierce when it takes over. It creates doubt, relentless worry, disappointment, greed, jealousy, and even anger.

It is hard to combat fear once it takes hold of the intellect. It's as if it erupts from some long-dormant volcano, spreading ash and hot molten emotions that destroy everything in its path. These molten emotions multiply layer upon layer of broken dreams, goals, and desires.

Fear creates suffering in all dimensions of our bodies, almost forming an indestructible wall for love to penetrate. Fear is cold. It cares little about whom or what is destroyed. It holds us down, keeping us captive from our own truth, from our love and our power.

Angela: Fear paralyzes me when I allow it to enter. Why do I allow it to enter my being, to infiltrate my mind, body, and soul? Why? What is the pattern that allows it to walk on, almost as if it enters under a false pretense and then shows its true, disturbing energy once inside?

It creeps slowly around, trying to find a vulnerable thought, word, or action. It remains undetected by my senses. Once it strikes, my true self hides, fearful of the wrath that may take place.

It seems this fear is ancient. Is it a memory from days long ago?

I ask myself what purpose fear has. How does it penetrate my undying love for others and my love for myself? What is fear's goal? Does it want control? It is like the devil of my mind.

Fear is a comfortable pattern I fall back into when love does not make sense. It is a comfortable pattern when love is so strong that it seems almost foreign to my senses. Fear is what I turn to when the vastness of love is so great that I lose track of where to start or what to say.

What Is the Root of My Thoughts?

Love sometimes seems like the vastness of the night sky. I can see some stars or a few planes passing by, and I am continuously wondering what is beyond the lights I see.

What is hidden in the depth of the night sky?

What is hidden within my Love?

Does the true definition of unconditional love reside there?

Is that where the vibration of love is?

How do I reach it?

Higher self: When you finally stop the thoughts and feel the vibration of Love, you can sink into an emotion that is not communicable. It takes some time for this new experience to sink into thought, but the vibration is so expansive and so pleasurable that you may never want to return to real life.

From this precept, love should only be felt and never put into words. When we try to put love into words, it becomes boxed in, limited, and confined. Love cannot fit into a label. It simply cannot fit. When we limit the feeling of love with our words, we constrain it. We try to take control of love and thereby allow fear to enter in undetected. It may feel as if fear is always waiting in the wings, eager to strike at any given moment. We assure you that if you operate from the premise of love, fear has no power.

What if we thought of love as emostringless? What if we did not try to define it but rather simply allowed it to morph and expand and ooze into every cell, every atom, every thought, and every word we used, every minute of every day? What then?

Love would become the only addiction we would ever need, an addiction without a need. It would be an addiction with never-ending nothingness — an addiction of bliss. What then?

Have you ever considered who you would be if love was your addiction? Not an addiction to the physical, mental, spiritual, or emotional form of earthly love. Rather, an addiction to the vastness of the vibration that unconditional love carries. Would you be pure, unconditional love?

Could you imagine what that would look like or feel like? When we allow ourselves to feel the vibration of love, not just the thought of love, vibrational healing happens naturally. In the world of love, everything is healed. We are whole. Without love, loneliness is overpowering and overbearing. Life in any form does not exist without love.

We have so much to learn in this third-dimensional form of being human, so many vibrations to experience of love. We have barely scratched the surface. We want you to experience true self-love and the power behind it. Love does conquer all, and we must allow it to enter the crevices of our bodies, minds, and souls.

For our sake, we must become love, true love — the unleashed, unboxed, and unlabeled version of love. We must be the uncensored version of love; then, we will know our purpose. For our real purpose is to be love. When we remember the love from which we came, there is no fear and there are no limits to what can be created.

We must become love, true love – the unleashed, unboxed, and unlabeled version of love.

Show Me

How Can I Stop Being So Afraid?

You can stop being afraid by loving who you are at the depth of your soul and not just on the surface of the physical body. Loving who we are includes our thoughts, actions, and emotions and not being afraid of them.

Fear comes from the walls you create as you are trying to stop yourself from being your authentic self. When we fear walking across the street because someone or something is there, then we will never go to the other side of the street. When we hold ourselves back, we miss opportunities for so much growth and expansion.

What if, on the other side of the street, is this book that held answers to your thought processes; yet, because of your fear of crossing the street you never allowed yourself to read this book? Therefore, you missed out on a vital opportunity for growth for your mental, emotional, and spiritual expansion. Because your soul wanted this experience and you allowed fear to control your decision to not cross the street, you ripped yourself from an experience that you may now have to repeat later in this life or in another lifetime, creating more pain and suffering along your journey.

When we allow fear to lead our life, we build walls around ourselves that are so thick and immense that it may take many lifetimes to break them down. When we allow fear to lead the way, we create habitual patterns and belief systems that are not for our highest good and joy. These fears hold us back from many experiences, growth, and expansions along our journey.

Your soul was incepted by love, and love is not equal to fear. Love is not afraid; rather, it is bold and compassionate. Love is kind and very strong. Love is powerful!

In order to divert fear, you must understand your love. Acknowledge the strength of your love. Acknowledge how powerful it is, and let it shine for the entire world to see, feel, smell, and hear. Give the world your gift of love. This is the most powerful you that exists.

Two things you can do to understand the power of your love:

1. **Write a letter to yourself everyday.** In this letter talk about your love. How powerful do you feel when you allow yourself to feel your love?

2. **Allow your soul's song to emerge.** Sit in meditation or go for a walk in nature. Create a peacefulness within you. Ask your soul to allow its song to emerge. Write it down, and sing it every day, creating a beautiful relationship between you and your song.

When we live our lives guided by our love, there is no room for fear. Step into your power of love, and live your life fearlessly, guided by divine joy.

ANGELA'S LETTER TO HERSELF

Dear Angela,

My love is sometimes timid, afraid to show itself, as it has experienced oppression for so many lifetimes. I knew at a soul level that coming to Earth this lifetime that I would be a bit handicapped because of my love and the vastness of it. I knew there would be a part of me that did not fit in this earthly plane, yet I chose to come. I know that my love is so deep that words cannot express it. I know that my love can be experienced, yet some shy away because of the intensity of it.

Because of these experiences with people, I tend to hold back my love or mask it with some other emotion. Sometimes, those emotions can be harsh. I sometimes show a lack of love just so I do not have to experience betrayal or love unreceived.

Love can be confusing, as it views everything as love. When I perceive something as hurtful, my love tells me to accept and forgive. This leaves me not understanding what love is, as my programming tells me not to accept everything as love. Yet, at a soul level, I know I should.

I have tried to wrap my brain around unconditional love; yet, at times my brain refuses to understand. Instead of understanding love, I try to *feel* love. There is no definition that equals the feeling I get from the vibrational experience of love.

I am choosing to accept the vibration of love without definition. I choose to experience love rather than to define it.

All my love,
Angela

Love
does not have
conditions.

Show Me What Does Forgiveness Mean?

Forgiveness means to stop putting limits and rules around your love. Forgiveness means to let go of self-judgment. When a mistake is made, forgive and let it go. You are not required to carry every mistake for your entire lifetime. When you attach yourself to your mistakes healing does not happen.

When you act in a way that does not reflect who you really want to be, forgive, and let it go. Create a new way that matches who you really want to be. Heal your repetition of any pattern that does not fit who you desire to be. Create new patterns, ones that make you feel awesome about who you are. Once you forgive yourself, do not go back to the same old patterns. You have to create new patterns that are more congruent with who you truly are.

Be kind to yourself through the process of forgiveness. When we are kind to ourselves, it leads us to a non-judgmental state of being. This is the state of being love.

Judgment continues to bind us to old habitual patterns. Once we get out of the routine of judgment, it is much easier for forgiveness to take place. When we have created patterns that are congruent with who we really are, we live in flow.

When we match our soul's intent, we stop seeing inequality. Rather, we see relevance according to the self. Now, I can hear you saying, doesn't that sound a bit too confident, almost egotistical? No, the perception of relating ego to self-love needs to change along with your forgiveness patterns. Living your life according to the self is the precise thing to do!

Angela: What if a person believes they are in flow with their soul, and yet they do cruel things to others?

Higher Self: The key word is "believes." When we are truly in touch with our soul, we remember we are of love, not something else. Love does have different vibrations or dimensions, but it does not have a polarity of cruelty to it.

In order to divert fear,
you must understand your love.

Show Me

Why Is Forgiveness Important for My Soul?

Forgiveness is for the self. It is for others only in the sense that when you forgive yourself you ultimately forgive all involved. If we must put it into words, forgiveness means something similar to the following:

> **Forgiveness:** *To review your part of what happened. Consider the incident, which you allowed yourself to take part in or to make a part of your emotional, mental, and sometimes physical body. Review what you created as your own.*

According to the online version of the Merriam-Webster dictionary, forgive means:

- to stop feeling anger toward (someone who has done something wrong)

- to stop blaming (someone)

- to stop feeling anger about (something): to forgive someone for (something wrong)

- to stop requiring payment of (money that is owed)

All of the versions above do include the self.

Let's take Angela's incident with her father when she was 12 years old as an example. At that time, he told her she was lazy. She still questions herself about this statement to this day. What part of these words and this suggestion did she take on and carry forward in her life?

If we become a witness to ourselves and take ourselves out of the physical body, moving to a higher level within our spiritual body, we can look down on the situation with a broader viewpoint. What can we logically conclude from this situation? We can see the motions unfolding and describe the scene from this new vantage point:

Angela has just arrived home from school. She is eating a piece of bread, sitting in a chair in the living room, and watching her favorite show, "Star Trek." Her father comes out of the bathroom, sees her sitting there watching TV, and tells her, "You're so lazy you stink."

He raises his hand in the air and gestures to hit her if she does not get up and move immediately. Angela does not know that her father is still suffering from a hangover, even though it is now nearly 4 o'clock in the afternoon. Fearing she will be hit, Angela rushes outside to do her daily chores.

Emotionally, what does Angela think and do? She has witnessed her father hitting her siblings before, although she has never been hit by him. The simple gesture reminds her of seeing her sibling being hit. It sends a message of fight or flight to her brain.

Her previous witnessing of hostile events has made a connection between pain and suffering, along with fear. Until she deals with the emotions that plague her, this same fight-or-flight response will be triggered each time she witnesses a similar event.

What emotions does Angela experience? She feels terror, guilt, embarrassment, a lack of trust, blame, and shame, just to name a few.

Those are six significant emotions to attach to the word, "lazy," and the raising of her father's hand. In order to deal with these emotions, they must first be released from the memory of her father's gesture and the past experience with him hitting a sibling. If this release does not occur, the emotions remain attached to the memory and are triggered sequentially. In order to forgive herself for taking on the emotions, Angela needs to separate the emotions from the events of the memory.

If Angela had understood the premise of unconditional love, she would not have taken her father's emotions or his current state of being and made it a part of her own experience. Instead, she would have allowed him to be in his own state of being miserable. She could have pushed back her father's energy, emotions, and words, recognizing that those were not hers to take from him.

When we come from unconditional love, we should not take another's emotions or words from them. We simply return these emotions back to them through the power of our love, because the experience belongs to them, not to you. The emotions do not belong to the one who is the target of another's projected shame. Those emotions belong to their owner.

Forgiveness seems very complex on the surface, because of all the emotions we attach to a particular memory. This complexity can be a result of conditioning, sometimes in the form of the repeated stuffing down of emotions for years, even decades.

When we can separate out the memory and look at the situation with a new perspective, we can recognize what happened logically and emotionally. We begin to understand how most of the time we simply took what someone else did or said and made it our own. Because emotions are complex, multidimensional, and can stack on top of one another, it seems to make the event even more dramatic.

When we forgive ourselves for taking on another's emotional state of being, we free ourselves, allowing the memory to simply be a memory without an emotional charge attached. If Angela would not have attached her own emotion to what she heard and seen by the gesture — or had she experienced what her father was experiencing at a vibrational level, she would have had an entirely different reaction.

Note from Angela: This is true, as I would have been empathic and almost sympathetic of my father's choices. I would have understood that what he was expressing was not actually a reflection of me or who I am. Rather, he was projecting onto me what he was feeling toward himself. I would have sent him unconditional love to help with his healing instead of responding in fear to his actions. The end result would have been much different for the both of us!

When we come from unconditional
love, we allow others to be
where they need to be
on their soul's journey.

Show Me

Why Is It Important to Forgive Myself?

Forgiveness is very important, almost as important as loving yourself. Why? Because when we forgive ourselves, we open and heal our mental and emotional bodies, restoring them to love.

When we forgive, we allow love to enter us, and healing begins to take place. We already know that love heals all. Through forgiveness, we open that door for love to enter. We open the door to freedom — freedom from all of our thoughts and from belief patterns that do not serve our higher purpose.

Forgiveness frees us from patterns that are not useful to us anymore. We let go of patterns that are possibly holding us back from our soul's journey. Forgiveness brings many freedoms at a mental and emotional level. This ability to expand at the mental and emotional level has been ignored for many centuries, and it is time to heal them. Not allowing the mental and emotional bodies to heal has kept the human in the rotating cycle of separation.

With forgiveness comes the healing of the belief pattern that you are separate from your spirit and from your love. When we forgive ourselves we heal thoughts, memories, and emotions, and we release cell memory. When we heal, we free ourselves from carrying these experiences into our future or other lifetimes.

All your bodies — the physical, mental, emotional, and spiritual bodies — work together, along with the elements, the sun, moon, and galaxies within which you live. Everything works harmoniously together. When we have a belief that separates that, it creates pain and suffering. So, forgiveness is very important.

A few things to do when working with forgiveness:

1. **Be kind to yourself.**

2. **Look at the big picture.**

3. **Take baby steps.**

Forgiveness may bring the illusion that it is not happening immediately. Some belief patterns do take more work to heal, depending on how ingrained they are. Stay with it, because as we have seen, forgiveness is important for your well-being in life.

When we forgive ourselves,
we open and heal our mental
and emotional bodies,
restoring them to love.

Show Me

How Can I Forgive When There's So Much to Forgive?

Oh, beautiful souls, from where we sit, there is nothing that is too overwhelming or terrifying to be forgiven. It is only the emotions that are attached to the memories that are overwhelming and terrifying, and those emotions can be transformed and transmuted; so, in reality, there is nothing to fear, because we are here to help with the fear. In fact, we can take it away from you if you so desire. All you have to do is ask your higher self to take away the fear.

You did not come to Earth to live a life of pain and suffering, you came to Earth to be love. If you were to take away your self-judgment, you would be able to view your situation in a different light. If you have not lived your life according to your soul's plan of love, then you have the ability to change your life now.

Detach from your emotions, and review the facts of your life. Then, forgive yourself. God / Spirit / Universe does not hold grudges for your actions, thoughts, or words. Allow yourself to be forgiven. Release the emotions, and allow them to detach from your memories. Make a plan to start a new you — one who lives according to your life's purpose and comes from a place of love.

A CHANNELED MESSAGE FROM ARCHANGEL METATRON

All things begin and end with Love. Love heals all wounds, all patterns and addictions — everything. When you ignore the signs and continue to lack self-love, you fall into the illusive trap of karmic patterns and behaviors. You have the gift of choice, so I ask, "Why are you not choosing love?"

I know love can be a scary emotion, especially when you are used to not having unconditional love for yourself. If you can get past the fear of how love reacts unconditionally to everything, you will experience life in a whole new way. The vastness of love is beautiful, yet love is very misunderstood. Loving yourself is not egotistical, as you may have been taught. Instead, it is humble.

Mother Teresa said it best: "When you are humble nothing will touch you, neither praise nor disgrace, because you know what you are."

Self-love is not praise; it is rather a form of care, grace, and joy. You need to change the way you think about self-love if you want to understand what it is to be humble. Being humble is the greatest sense of self-love, the greatest gift you have been given.

When you do not acknowledge your own love for you, you do not know who you are. You follow the crowd instead of standing in your own wisdom and truth, confident in your own power. When you ignore your own wisdom and truth, you create your pain and suffering.

You have a choice. Choose love over pain every time.

Love is strong, encouraging, and kind. It makes you feel as if you are home among the vastness of the universe. Nothing can penetrate it or break it down.

Go within, and feel the love your soul has for you. If it is too strong, then visit your soul often to get accustomed to the feeling of love. Do not fear the overwhelming joy that unconditional, true love can bring to you. You are very deserving of its beauty.

Namaste

Show Me What Else Do I Need to Understand about Forgiveness?

When we talk about forgiveness, there seems to be a negative impact associated with the word. There is a sense of having to give up something or give into someone else. This is part of the illusion of your thought process, as forgiveness is only for the self.

When you forgive yourself for an action you took, a thought you had, or words you said or did not say, you are only forgiving your own actions, thoughts, or words, not someone else's. You are not responsible for another's actions, thoughts, or words, nor can you force someone else to forgive you. Each person is responsible for his or her own actions, thoughts, and words. Each person must choose forgiveness.

The only person you give in to is yourself. Isn't that the point? When we give into ourselves, we recognize the patterns of our thinking, our actions, and our words. It is only when we become aware of our patterns that we recognize how such patterns are harming the self. You have the ability to change these patterns.

Forgiveness means becoming aware of the patterns and then taking action to change those patterns so we eliminate self-harm. So, there is no giving in or giving up anything to someone else. Rather, there is the beginning or continuation of self-love.

Fear comes in because of our growing awareness of just how much we do hurt ourselves. Self-forgiveness, along with self-love, can be scary. This is especially true if we have grown up in a family and with societal rules that have taught us not to love ourselves.

We do not live in ego when we come from a place of love, because the ego does not promote love. The soul does. Go ahead and live by your soul's rules about love. You have so much love! Keeping it tucked inside, not allowing it out to be shared with yourself and others, is simply a transgression.

Here are three things you can do to forgive yourself:

1. **When you review the action or thought** associated with a particular incident, look at the big picture, not simply your point of view. Imagine the other person's point of view as well.

2. **Identify the underlying feeling or emotion.** Is it guilt, shame, or blame? Or is it something else?

3. **Create another outcome** — one that is for your higher self. There are four steps you can follow to do so.

    - Consider whether your perception is really accurate after reviewing the bigger picture.

    - Make amends for your action in the situation.

What Else Do I Need to Understand about Forgiveness?

- Forgive yourself for your part in the situation. Release it.

- Trust that you are healing your wounds and learn from the experience.

Take small steps. As you do, the overwhelming and terrifying feelings will not rise up to block you as you give yourself permission to heal. These small steps help you to move along your soul's journey in grace.

The only person
you give in to
is yourself.

Show Me

How Can I Forgive Myself When I Continue to Mess Up?

You didn't create your patterns overnight, and you will not create new patterns to correct the old ones overnight. So be kind to yourself. Try not to judge, because when we make a judgment we take two steps back.

Instead of judging, simply say to yourself. "I'm okay. How can I change this pattern?" You might also ask:

What action, thought, or word can I change to heal this pattern for my highest good?

What do I need to learn from my patterns?

When we go into a state of judgment, it is as if we open the door to relentless anxiety and depression. We then fall back into the very comfortable patterns that we are trying to change. So, with all your power, try to stay away from and out of a judgmental state of being.

When trying to change a pattern, your first task should be to take an action step to create a new pattern and a new way of being. With action steps we create new thoughts, new feelings, and new words. Action steps toward change create a domino affect, and it becomes easier to create new patterns once the affect begins.

Now, just because you have a setback now and then does not mean you are not creating new patterns. We are creatures of habit, and it may take time to change. Just continue to create change, which is the point. Creating a difference in your usual way of being is forgiveness, one small step after another.

One way to know if your patterns are changing is to keep a record of how you are changing. This gives the logical brain some concrete evidence that the action steps you are taking are really working. The following is a way to record change; however, we encourage you to create your own new pattern of recording your changes.

Maybe you will find a pattern that works for you through art or doodling, singing, sitting in meditation, or creating a video. The possibilities are endless.

A few ways to know you are creating new patterns:

1. **Keep a record** of the patterns you are trying to change. The record may be mental or written.

2. **Notice how often a particular pattern occurs.** By keeping a written record, you can witness how far apart these incidents become and know that change is happening.

3. **Rejoice with every new pattern** that comes into your awareness. Be happy with who you are becoming.

4. **Trust that you are healing you.** Allow love to enter.

With action steps,
we create new thoughts,
new feelings, and new words.

Show Me What If I Know I Have Harmed Someone?

Remember we talked previously about love and how it heals everything? Love who you are, no matter your choices. This statement has been repeated many times throughout this book so you will remember it.

Many humans harm themselves every day, yet they think nothing of it. They go on with their day as if nothing happened. Ask yourself what it was you needed to learn when you made the choice to harm someone.

We all make mistakes or what we perceive to be mistakes. In reality, these mistakes may be lessons or experiences, which we need to have in order to learn and expand. This does not mean the choices we make to harm others or ourselves are accepted here on Earth or anywhere else. There is a very fine line, and there are rules to keep people safe and responsible for their actions. The earthly laws of natural and logical consequences are in place to protect others as well as yourself.

My point is this, even though we make choices to harm, we still have the ability and power to forgive. God / Universe / Spirit does not put conditions on forgiveness or love; so, therefore, neither should you.

Forgiveness comes into your awareness so that you can learn to forgive. Learn from your lessons or experiences, do not trap yourself in your patterns. Forgive yourself, and make choices that are for your soul's highest good.

Now, we want to address harm. We know that in a polar society, harm exists. Harm is a choice. Harm does not necessarily equal evil.

When we say harmful things or do harmful acts to others or ourselves with the resulting emotions of regret, anger, shame, or blame, we need to forgive ourselves immediately. When we forgive immediately, the brain in not able to come in and start rationalizing away what we said or what we have done, creating an escape by replacing our actions with words like blame or shame. When we go right to forgiveness, we heal ourselves and everyone involved as soon as the act is over. This creates a space for love to enter, allowing the experience to be experienced at a soul level and without judgment.

It is judgment that creates shame and blame. Shame and blame make it much harder for forgiveness to happen, because we have created scenarios in our minds that attach to other memories and create even bigger problems. When we do not go instantly to forgiveness and allow the brain to judge, then we add more emotions and feelings to the pile of things for which we need to forgive ourselves. This merely creates more pain and suffering.

We are not telling you to refrain from choosing harm, as we know there is a valuable lesson for you behind your choice. Rather, we are suggesting you forgive instantly and without judgment when you do make such a choice. Part of the reason you choose to come to Earth is to experience different things that are not experienced anywhere else in the galaxies. We do ask that you choose wisely. Choosing harm is not something we recommend; however, when you choose it, please forgive!

Do not trap yourself in your patterns.

Show Me
What If I Do Not Think I Have Anything to Forgive

If you have no one or nothing to forgive then, my friend, you are one step ahead of life. If you truly do not have anything to forgive, one of two possibilities exists. Either you are doing the work of forgiveness as you live or your ego is ruling the way you live.

If, in fact, you are truly living your life and doing the emotional work along the way, we applaud you. This is the easiest of ways to live. Healing the emotional body is vital in living a life of freedom, because, as we have stated before, pain and suffering results when the emotional body has not been healed. Healing the emotional body can either be done as you are living in present time or at the end of life when the transition process occurs as a life review.

There is tremendous soul growth if you are able to heal the emotional body as you are living. Because when you heal in human form, you use all your bodies as one body. All bodies are then healed. When you heal in present time, you are healing cell memory as well as spiritual and emotional memory.

When you heal in physical form rather than spirit form, it is very meaningful and loving as the soul experiences healing in another form. This is of great importance to the soul. The soul realizes it does not need to carry those emotions with it any longer, because those wounds are healed. This forgiveness creates more space for the remembering of divine love to enter into your human experience.

If you have chosen to allow the ego to be in control this lifetime, then more than likely forgiveness of the self is not in your awareness, at least for the time during which the ego is in control. We offer that everything can change. Please keep in mind that you are the one who makes the choices in your life, and the work of forgiveness is very much a choice.

There is no right or wrong way of being, there is only an experience. So if you think there is nothing to forgive, then there is nothing. You should not spend hours worrying or questioning what you need to forgive or if you have forgiveness or healing to do. If you do indeed have forgiveness work to do, trust that it will come into your awareness and that you have the ability to so.

There is no right or wrong way
of being. There is only
an experience.

Show Me What Are the Actual Steps of Forgiveness?

There is not a concrete plan when we talk about forgiveness and how you do it. There is not a tablet of stone in some elusive place that gives you step-by-step instructions as to what action steps are needed to forgive yourself.

We offer a few things to consider on your journey of forgiveness:

First, allow your actions, words, and thoughts to constantly be in your awareness. When you live in the present moment, you are aware. At such times, there is no work of remembering required to live in the here and now.

If you are constantly worrying, you are living in the future. If you are depressed, you are living in the past. When you are joyful and filled with grace and gratitude, you are living in the present moment. We recommend the present. Living in the present moment is living in a continuous state of awareness. This leads you to a place where choices are in your conscious awareness and you become better able to choose what will keep you in flow with the life you have chosen to live.

Second, when you become aware of an emotion trying to arise, allow it to rise. So many times, we pretend it is not there. Or we say to ourselves, "I can't deal with this now." We continue to stuff it down, creating greater pain. We ask you, "Why can't you deal with your emotions when they arise?" If you are living in the present moment, in a state of full awareness, you will naturally deal with things as they arise. In the present moment, you allow more of your authentic self to emerge.

Third, allow yourself to forgive. Discern what forgiveness really means for you and allow yourself to heal. You are the only one who can heal you. You have been given free will, which puts you in the driver's seat of your life. The driver of your life is not God / Universe / Spirit. It is you. You make your choices. You are not a puppet being controlled. You are love in many forms.

Fourth, when you do the emotional work of forgiveness, do not hold on to any part of it. Set yourself free from your perceptions, your emotions, and your thoughts. You are not bound to hold on to your emotions or memories with a ball and chain. There is freedom in forgiveness. Once it is done, allow love to enter.

Love heals all!

Love is the answer to all forgiveness that is needed.

We ask that you discover your own way of forgiveness. You are the master of your life, and we encourage you to step into the role of master. Create your own actions steps. There is no right or wrong way to forgive. There are only experiences.

Lastly, live as you want to be. Free yourself from your patterns that no longer serve you and from limiting perception, through love and forgiveness.

REMEMBER: YOU ARE LOVE!

What Are the Actual Steps of Forgiveness?

There is freedom
in forgiveness.

Next Steps

Now that you've read this book, you may be wondering where you go from here. How do you stay on track, remembering your power through self-love and forgiveness? I suggest you work at your own pace. Some will work faster at forgiveness than others. All is perfectly well, and you are where you need or desire to be. Continue to practice the exercises in this book that work best for you.

If you would like personal assistance along your path to self-love and forgiveness, please visit my website at http://angelablaha.com. Visit the "Services" tab, and choose the best service to help you along on your journey. If you are not sure which service will provide you with what you most need, then simply send me an e-mail at angelablaha005@gmail.com. Together, we will establish what is for your highest good and joy.

I also provide a variety of classes, retreats, and private sessions. Information on these can be found on my website. Click the "Events" tab to learn more about upcoming events.

Be sure to download your **Show Me Meditation Kit**, which includes audio files of the meditations in this book. Use them as often as desired to connect more deeply with your higher self.

Thank you for allowing me the opportunity to share a portion of your journey.

About the Author

Angela Blaha is a transformational teacher, healer, and personal coach who supports those who desire emotional healing to overcome obstacles to greater joy and fulfillment. She helps her clients transform thoughts, feelings, and emotions to create new patterns that allow them to decrease stress and increase optimism and fulfill their dreams and desires. She is the author of the *Show Me* book series and enjoys leading classes and retreats.

Angela has studied extensively with Deepak Chopra and serves as a Primordial Sound Meditation Instructor with the Chopra Center. In addition, she has studied Feng Shui with Katie Weber and is a certified Master Consultant in Classical Feng Shui. She is also a certified Life and Wellness Coach with the International Coaching Federation.

She is a Level III Master Akashic Records Practitioner, a registered hypnotherapist with the National Guild of Hypnotherapists, a Reiki master and teacher, and has studied with The Foundation for Shamanic Studies. She holds a bachelor's degree in psychology and a master's degree in psychology and counseling in education.

www.ingramcontent.com/pod-product-compliance
Lightning Source LLC
Chambersburg PA
CBHW071625080526
44588CB00010B/1268